WESTCHESTER PUBLIC LIB

P9-EMN-150

EAT SMART

VEGETABLES

Louise Spilsbury

Heinemann Library
Chicago, Illinois

© 2009 Heinemann Library
an imprint of Capstone Global Library, LLC
Chicago, Illinois

Customer Service 888-454-2279

Visit our website at www.heinemannraintree.com

All rights reserved. No part of this publication may be reproduced or transmitted in any form or by any means, electronic or mechanical, including photocopying, recording, taping, or any information storage and retrieval system, without permission in writing from the publisher.

Printed and bound in China by CTPS

13 12 11 10 09
10 9 8 7 6 5 4 3 2 1

Library of Congress Cataloging-in-Publication Data
Spilsbury, Louise.
  Vegetables / Louise Spilsbury. -- 1st ed.
     p. cm. -- (Eat smart)
  Includes bibliographical references and index.
  ISBN 978-1-4329-1814-9 (hc) -- ISBN 978-1-4329-1821-7 (pb) 1. Vegetables--Juvenile literature. 2. Cookery (Vegetables)--Juvenile literature. I. Title.
  TX401.S65 2009
  641.6'51--dc22
                                 2008045279

Acknowledgments
We would like to thank the following for permission to reproduce photographs: © Alamy pp. 6 (John Glover), 7 (Harryhaussen), 17 (vario images GmbH & Co. KG); © Getty Images p. 11 (Iconica/Steve Satushek); © iStockphoto pp. 1-32 background images; © Pearson Education Ltd/MM Studios pp. 10, 16, 21, 24, 25 top, 25 bottom, 27 top, 27 middle, 27 bottom, 28, 29 top, 29 bottom; © Photolibrary pp. 4, 9 (Digital Vision), 13, 14 (Imagesource), 18, 19; © Science Photo Library pp. 8 (Adam Hart-Davis), 12 (Nigel Cattlin/Holt Studios International), 15 (Susumu Nishinaga); © StockFood UK pp. 5 (FoodPhotogr. Eising), 20 (Foodcollection).

Cover photograph reproduced with permission of © Corbis (moodboard).

Every effort has been made to contact copyright holders of material reproduced in this book. Any omissions will be rectified in subsequent printings if notice is given to the publishers.

Disclaimer
All the Internet addresses (URLs) given in this book were valid at the time of going to press. However, due to the dynamic nature of the Internet, some addresses may have changed, or sites may have changed or ceased to exist since publication. While the author and publishers regret any inconvenience this may cause readers, no responsibility for any such changes can be accepted by either the author or the publishers.

CONTENTS

Some words are shown in bold, **like this**. You can find out what they mean by looking in the glossary.

WHAT ARE VEGETABLES?

Vegetables are plants, or parts of plants, that people grow and use for food. We eat vegetables in many different ways, sometimes raw and sometimes cooked. We often eat vegetables as a part of dinner. This is because, unlike fruits, most vegetables do not taste sweet. A few vegetables have a natural sweetness, and these are sometimes used in desserts, such as carrots in carrot cake and pumpkin in pumpkin pie.

Why is it smart to eat vegetables?

Vegetables are rich in **nutrients**. Nutrients are substances that the human body needs so that it can grow, develop properly, and stay healthy. Eating vegetables helps to protect the body against some forms of disease and keeps the heart working well. Vegetables also help the body to make the **energy** it needs to be active and carry out all body processes, including breathing.

⬆ Today, most supermarkets sell vegetables grown from local farmers as well as those shipped from all over the world.

World of vegetables

There are hundreds of different kinds of vegetables across the world. Some are linked to the cooking of particular countries or regions. For example, bok choy is a leafy green vegetable used mostly in Chinese cooking. Okra is a long green vegetable with a slightly fuzzy skin that is often used in Indian, African, and Caribbean meals. Yams, which look like long, pointed potatoes, are very popular in Africa.

This selection of colorful carrots, peppers, and other vegetables has been sliced and cooked in oil to make a Chinese stir-fry.

Sea vegetables

Some kinds of seaweed are eaten as vegetables, too. Nori, kelp, and wakame are sold dried. People usually soak and then boil or fry them as part of a Japanese meal. Agar seaweed is used to thicken foods such as soup, salad dressing, and desserts.

History of vegetables

Most of the vegetables we eat today first grew as wild plants long ago. People began to plant and grow vegetables on farms about 11,000 years ago. Farmers first grew spinach in the area that is now Iran in the Middle East, and they first grew carrots in Asia around Afghanistan.

Explorers and traders gradually took vegetables across the world, from the regions where they first grew to other countries. For example, the Spanish explorer Christopher Columbus (1451–1506) took corn plants and tomatoes from South America and peppers from the West Indies to countries in Europe.

Purple carrots?

Up until the 1600s, most carrots were purple, white, yellow, or red. Then, Dutch scientists and farmers began to experiment and to **crossbreed** yellow carrot plants with red varieties. They produced the first orange carrot as a tribute to the House of Orange. These rulers' symbolic color was orange.

Today, some people are becoming interested in trying old varieties of vegetables that have long been forgotten, such as purple, yellow, and white carrots.

Although plants such as peppers and chilis grow naturally in tropical places, farmers can grow them in cold climates by keeping them in heated greenhouses.

Vegetables and climate

Almost all plants need soil, water, and light to grow, but some vegetables grow better in different **climates**. For example, plants such as peppers and chilis grow best in warm, damp places. Brussels sprouts need long cold spells to grow well and can even survive frost and snow. Some kinds of vegetables, such as beans, can grow in a wide variety of climates all over the world.

Some vegetables, such as carrots, grow pretty much all year round. Other vegetables only grow in certain seasons. In many parts of the United States, for example, asparagus grows in late spring, and sweet corn is available from about July through the early fall.

WHERE DO VEGETABLES COME FROM?

Few vegetable plants are eaten whole. We mainly eat certain parts of a plant, such as the roots, leaves, stalks, or stems, and even the fruit and flowers. The plant parts we eat come in different shapes and sizes on different kinds of plants. For example, we eat the single large root of the carrot plant, while we eat the large **edible** green leaves of the spinach plant.

What are the parts of a plant?

Each part of a plant does a different job.

- Roots hold a plant in the ground and take in water from the soil.
- Shoots and stems grow above ground. They hold up the plant's leaves and flowers.
- Leaves make the plant's food.
- The plant's flowers make seeds.
- The fruit is the part of the plant that grows around the seeds to protect them until they are fully developed. Then the seeds fall to the ground and grow into new plants.

Even though potatoes are called root vegetables, the potatoes that we eat are actually swollen underground stems used by the plant to store food. Potato plant roots are small and inedible.

Why don't we eat the whole plant?

While some parts of a vegetable plant are nutritious, other parts can make us sick. We can eat the roots of the potato plant, but all of the other parts of the plant would give people stomach pain and make them sick if eaten. Some vegetable plants can be eaten whole. We can eat the feathery green leaves at the top of the carrot plant as well as its root.

To harvest bunches of carrots, a machine loosens the soil so that the carrot roots can be pulled out by their leafy tops.

Giant vegetables

The edible root of a tropical yam plant can be up to 6–9 feet (2–3 meters) long and weigh 50 pounds (168 kilograms) or more! Don't expect to see these monsters in the stores, though, because most yams are harvested when they weigh about 2 pounds (1 kilogram).

Vegetables above ground

Some vegetables are the parts of plants that grow above ground. Vegetables that are leaves of plants include Brussels sprouts, cabbage, lettuce, Swiss chard, kale, bok choy, and spinach. Some vegetables, such as cauliflower and broccoli, are unopened flower **buds**. Some vegetables, including celery, bamboo shoots, and asparagus, are the stalks and shoots of plants.

Cauliflower and broccoli tops consist of many white and green flower buds, called florets.

Vegetables below ground

We use different underground plant parts as vegetables. Carrots, sweet potatoes, cassava, and parsnip are plant roots. Yams and sweet potatoes are **tubers**. Tubers are thickened underground stems or roots that store food for the plant. **Bulb** vegetables include garlic, leeks, onions, shallots, and green onions. Bulbs consist of fleshy, underground leaves or scales that store food over winter, ready to grow new plants in the spring.

When is a fruit a vegetable?

In scientific terms, some vegetables are actually fruits because they hold the plant's seeds. We call them vegetables because they are not sweet and we often eat them as a part of dinner. Fruits that we eat as vegetables include eggplants, avocados, chilis, peppers, and tomatoes.

Pods are a different kind of fruit. They are like green cases that contain a plant's seeds. We can eat both the pod and seeds of kidney beans, okra, and and some other pea plants.

Squash are fruits that we eat as vegetables. Varieties of squash include zucchini, cucumbers, butternut squash, and pumpkins.

What is the world's most expensive vegetable?

Mushrooms are a type of **fungus**. People eat many varieties of mushrooms as vegetables, including button, portobello, oyster, porcini, and shiitake mushrooms. Another type of fungus, the truffle, is the world's most expensive vegetable. In 2007, a single truffle, weighing 3.3 pounds (1.5 kilograms), sold for over $330,000!

WHY ARE VEGETABLES GOOD FOR YOU?

Vegetables are good for us because they are sources of important **nutrients** such as **vitamins** and **minerals**, and other substances such as **fiber**. The body needs these things to stay healthy.

Why do plants contain nutrients?

Plants make some of their own nutrients by a process called **photosynthesis**. Plants take in water from the soil through their roots, and they absorb a gas called carbon dioxide through holes in their leaves. Plants use **energy** from the sunlight that shines on their leaves to combine the carbon dioxide and water. This creates sugars that the plant uses as food. Water entering plant roots contains other nutrients from the soil. The plant uses all these nutrients to grow and stay healthy.

Food made in a plant's leaves using photosynthesis travels around the plant in tubes to nourish all the other parts of the plant.

Why are vitamins so important?

When we eat plants, we take in nutrients such as vitamins from the plants. People need vitamins to grow, to develop properly, and to survive. People who eat plenty of vegetables are less likely to get serious diseases such as **diabetes**, heart disease, and some forms of **cancer**.

You cannot make all the vitamins your body needs. To stay supplied with a healthy supply of vitamins, you have to take vitamins into your body every day through the food that you eat.

Vegetables and water

Vegetables are also good for us because they contain a lot of water. Some leafy green vegetables, such as lettuce, are up to 96 percent water! Water is the most important nutrient of all. The human body is mostly made up of water, but we lose some water every day when we **urinate** and sweat. We need to keep the body's water levels well supplied, and eating fresh vegetables helps us to do that.

Our bodies can only work properly if we keep our water levels well supplied. We all need to take in plenty of water every day, and eating juicy vegetables with high water content really helps.

Vitamin groups

There are two main groups of vitamins: fat **soluble** and water soluble. Vitamins A, D, E, and K are fat soluble. They are transported around the body in fat. Any vitamins that are not used immediately are stored in the **liver** and in body fat. Some vitamins, including B vitamins and vitamin C, are transported around the body in water. Water-soluble vitamins that are not used pass out of the body in urine. That is why we need to eat foods containing these vitamins every day.

Vitamin	What is it good for?	What vegetables is it found in?
Vitamin A	Good for eyesight, healthy skin, and bone growth, and helps to protect against infections	Carrots, butternut squash, sweet potatoes, and tomatoes
B vitamins	Help turn food into energy and maintain blood **cells**	Beans, peas, and leafy green vegetables
Vitamin C	Helps keep gums, teeth, and muscles healthy; helps the body to fight infections and to heal when wounded	Broccoli, sweet red peppers, cabbage, and tomatoes
Vitamin E	Keeps body **tissues** healthy and protects them from damage that can result in diseases such as cancer and heart disease	Leafy green vegetables
Vitamin K	Helps the blood to **clot** during bleeding	Broccoli and leafy green vegetables

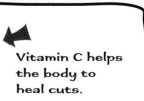

Vitamin C helps the body to heal cuts.

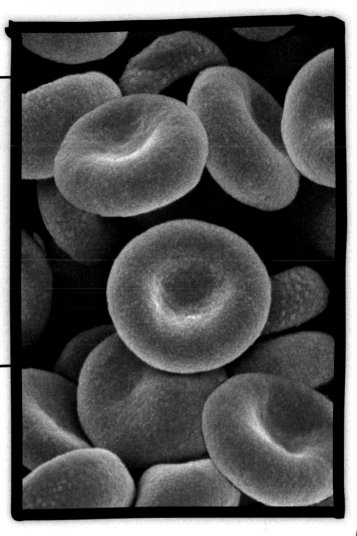

The mineral iron helps to make red blood cells, shown enlarged here, which carry **oxygen** throughout the body. All body cells use oxygen to release energy from digested food. Vegetables that are good sources of iron include beans and peas, broccoli, and spinach.

Minerals in vegetables

The minerals we get from vegetables are important to our health.

- Calcium from leafy green vegetables such as broccoli and spinach helps the body grow strong bones and teeth.
- Magnesium in sweet corn, peas, and mushrooms helps the body release energy from food and helps the muscles work well.
- The body uses iron from vegetables such as spinach, spring greens, and bok choy to make red blood cells.
- The mineral potassium helps the heart to pump blood around the body. It is found in sweet potatoes, tomato paste, tomato sauce, spinach, and squash.

Why do we need fiber?

Fiber helps you to feel full so that you don't snack on unhealthy foods between meals. It also helps to keep the **digestive system** healthy, and it may reduce the risk of getting certain types of cancer and heart disease. Plants grow strands of fiber to give them strength and shape. We get a lot of fiber by eating vegetables.

Keeping things moving

Fiber passes through the digestive system without being broken down. Instead, it soaks up water, thereby making food waste softer so it passes out of the body more easily. This is important because it is unhealthy to have food waste in the body for too long. Baked potato skins, celery, and leafy green vegetables are especially good sources of fiber.

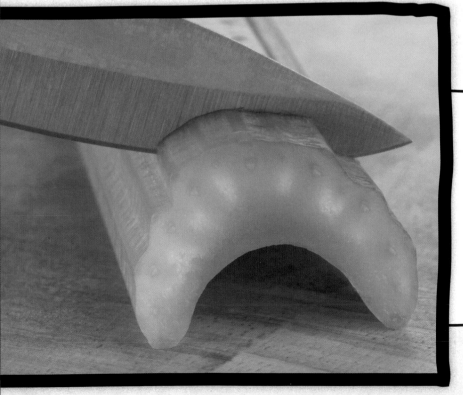

Many vegetables, including celery, are high in fiber, which helps make you feel full and keeps your digestive system working well.

Starchy vegetables such as sweet corn and peas give the body energy, while B vitamins from beans and leafy green vegetables help the body release energy from food.

Vegetable variety

Different vegetables contain different combinations of nutrients. To get all the nutrients you need to be healthy, select vegetables from each of the following five groups several times per week:

- dark green vegetables such as broccoli, spinach, and lettuce
- orange vegetables, including carrot, pumpkin, sweet potato, and winter squash, which are a good source of vitamin A
- dry beans and peas, including split peas, lentils, kidney beans, and chickpeas, which are excellent sources of **protein**. Protein provides the raw materials the body needs to grow and stay well, as well as other nutrients such as iron.
- **starchy** vegetables such as sweet corn, yams, potatoes, and peas, which provide **carbohydrates**, an excellent source of energy
- other vegetables such as bean sprouts, cauliflower, celery, cucumbers, eggplant, mushrooms, okra, onions, and zucchini.

WHAT IS THE BEST WAY TO EAT VEGETABLES?

Fresh, frozen, chilled, canned, and dried vegetables are all good for you. The important thing is to eat a variety of vegetables, because this makes meals more interesting and nutritious.

Fresh vegetables

Vegetables gradually lose some **nutrients**, such as **vitamin** C, after they have been picked. The longer they have been traveling or stored, the more their nutrient levels will drop. To get the maximum nutrients, choose vegetables that are in season, as these will be at their peak flavor, and eat them soon after buying. Some fresh vegetables keep longer than others. Root vegetables such as carrots keep for a week or two in a cool, dark place. Lettuce leaves may only keep for a few days, even when stored chilled in a refrigerator.

Taking the time to make a plate of vegetables look appealing can tempt people to eat more of them.

Preserved vegetables

Preserved vegetables keep longer than fresh ones and are a good way to try vegetables that are out of season or not grown locally. Generally, vegetables are canned, bottled, or frozen immediately after being picked, when their nutrient content is at its peak. Drying vegetables to preserve them can result in loss of some vitamin C, but other nutrients are retained.

Choose canned vegetables that do not contain added sugar and salt, because too much salt and sugar is unhealthy. ➡

Fast freeze!

Beginning about 1912, Clarence Birdseye experimented with how to freeze food successfully. While on a fishing trip to Canada, he realized that by leaving fish on the ice, the fish froze so quickly that crystals didn't form to spoil its taste and texture. Today, peas and many other kinds of vegetables are frozen within two to three hours of being harvested.

Why do we wash vegetables?

Washing vegetables removes dirt from the field where they grew and **microorganisms** that may have gotten onto the vegetables while they were being transported. Rub vegetables with your hands or a small brush under clean, cold running water. Peeling vegetables also removes surface dirt, but do not peel too thickly, because many nutrients are stored just below the skin in some vegetables.

Making sure vegetables are washed or peeled properly is especially important when you plan to eat them raw.

Cooking vegetables

Vegetables are naturally low in fat and salt, both of which can be unhealthy if you have too much of them, so the way you prepare vegetables matters. The healthiest way to cook vegetables is steaming. When you cook vegetables in boiling water, some nutrients soak out of the vegetables into the water. Roasting and frying vegetables is fine occasionally, but try to use only small amounts of oil or butter. Cheese and cream sauces or salad dressings may add fat and salt to a meal, so eat only small amounts of these.

Many vegetables taste good raw, cut into chunks, or with a dip or dressing. Try yogurt or low-fat dressings with raw broccoli, red and green peppers, carrots, celery sticks, or cauliflower.

Top tips

Here are some ways to get more vegetables into your diet.

- Add vegetables such as lettuce and tomatoes to sandwiches or have salad for lunch.

- Include chopped vegetables in soups, stews, and pasta sauces.

- Always have vegetables or salad with dinner.

- Have a vegetable main dish such as a vegetable stir-fry or soup sometimes.

- Add vegetables such as sliced mushrooms, peppers, and onions to pizza toppings.

- Keep chunks of prepared vegetables, such as carrot and celery, in the refrigerator as snacks.

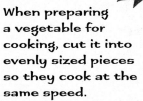

When preparing a vegetable for cooking, cut it into evenly sized pieces so they cook at the same speed.

HOW MANY VEGETABLES SHOULD YOU EAT?

Vegetables are a very important part of a healthy diet, and you should eat at least five portions of fruits and vegetables a day. You can eat vegetables with your lunch, in sandwiches, as snacks and, of course, as part of your dinner.

What is a portion of vegetables?

One portion of vegetables weighs 3 ounces (80 grams) after you have removed all the parts you cannot eat, such as skin or peel. This works out to roughly three tablespoons of chopped cooked vegetables per portion, or one cereal-sized bowl of salad, or two tablespoons of dry beans and peas. But don't worry too much about the exact size of a portion—just try to eat good amounts and a variety of different kinds of vegetables every day.

A balanced diet

Vegetables are only one of the foods you need to eat to be healthy. A balanced diet contains a variety of foods that together provide all the **nutrients** people need to be healthy. The Eatwell plate diagram (opposite) shows the types and proportions of foods needed for a balanced diet. It shows that people should eat:

- lots of fruits and vegetables
- plenty of grains and other **starchy carbohydrate** foods, such as bread, rice, pasta, and potatoes
- some milk and dairy foods
- some meat, fish, eggs, beans, and other non-dairy sources of **protein**
- just a small amount of foods and drinks that are high in fat or sugar.

Top tip

Even if you eat more than one portion of a particular type of vegetable, it still only counts as one per day. It is important to eat a variety of different types of vegetables to get the range of nutrients needed for good health.

Don't forget to drink plenty of water, too. Try to drink about six to eight glasses (40 fluid ounces) of fluid a day.

The "MyPyramid" food pyramid shows the proportion of food from each food group you should eat to achieve a healthy, balanced diet. This takes into account everything you eat, including snacks.

Vegetable Recipes

Vegetable stir-fry with noodles

Cooking vegetables quickly in a small amount of oil in a hot pan ensures they retain all their color, **nutrients**, and taste. This stir-fry should serve four people for dinner.

Ingredients

- 1 garlic clove
- 1 green pepper
- 1 yellow pepper
- 1 carrot
- 1 onion
- 1 cup (100 g) broccoli
- 1 cup (115 g) snap peas
- 1 tablespoon peanut oil or sunflower oil
- 2 tablespoons soy sauce
- 2-inch (5-cm) piece of fresh ginger root
- Noodles for four people (try **whole wheat** noodles for added **fiber**)

Equipment

- Wok or large, flat-bottomed saucepan
- Large saucepan for noodles
- Colander to strain noodles
- Chopping board
- Knives
- Garlic crusher
- Grater
- Wooden spoon for stirring

WHAT YOU DO

1 Prepare all the vegetables before you start to cook. Peel and crush the garlic. Peel and grate the ginger. Peel and slice the onion and carrot into little strips (like big matchsticks). Slice the green pepper and the yellow pepper into strips, too. Cut the broccoli into little florets or pieces. Wash the snap peas.

An adult should always help you when you use sharp knives and cook with oil, as in this recipe.

2 Heat the oil in a wok or large, flat-bottomed saucepan. Fry the onion, ginger, and garlic for 3 minutes. Add the peppers, then stir and fry for 3 minutes more.

3 Add the broccoli florets, snap peas, and carrots. Stir in the soy sauce. Continue to stir and fry for another 5 minutes, or until all the vegetables are just cooked. (If the vegetables start to stick, add a tablespoon of water.)

4 Cook the noodles according to the instructions on their package and make sure they are ready to serve with the vegetables as soon as the vegetables are cooked.

Baked sweet potato with pineapple

Sweet potatoes are an excellent source of **vitamins** A, B, and C and contain useful **minerals**, too. This recipe tastes great served with a green salad or cooked green vegetables such as broccoli and leeks.

Ingredients

- 6 sweet potatoes
- Butter or cooking oil
- 4 fl oz. (110 mL) orange juice
- 3 ¾ tablespoons butter
- ¾ teaspoon salt
- 8-oz. (225-g) can of crushed pineapple, drained

Equipment

- Baking sheet
- Knife
- Spoon
- Measuring cups and spoons
- Can opener
- Medium-sized mixing bowl
- Wooden spoon

WHAT YOU DO

1 Preheat the oven to 375°F (180°C). Use a vegetable brush to scrub the sweet potato skins under running water.

2 Use paper towels or parchment paper to spread some butter or oil over the baking sheet. This will make the baking sheet slightly greasy so the potatoes won't stick to it when they cook. Put the sweet potatoes on the sheet and bake in the oven for 1 hour.

3 Use an oven mitt to take the sheet out of the oven. Leave the sweet potatoes to cool slightly. Then slice the potatoes open lengthwise. Use a spoon to scoop the potato flesh out of each potato skin and into a mixing bowl. Leave enough flesh in the skin so that it is a firm shell.

4 Use a wooden spoon to mix the orange juice, butter, and salt with the sweet potato flesh. Stir until the mixture is fluffy. Then stir the pineapple into the mixture.

5 Carefully fill the potato skins with the mixture.

6 Put the potatoes back on the baking sheet and put them in the oven again for another 10 minutes.

7 Remove from the oven and serve.

Vegetable soup

Vegetable soup is a good way to eat a mixture of vegetables. You could try this recipe with different vegetables such as cabbage or mushrooms. Experiment with different vegetables until you find your favorite mix.

Ingredients

- 1 onion
- 1 carrot
- 1 leek
- 1 potato
- 2 celery sticks
- 1 3/4 tbsp (25 g) butter
- 1/4 cup (25 g) flour
- 1 vegetable stock cube
- 17 fl oz. (500 mL) boiling water

Equipment

- Chopping board
- Knife
- Vegetable peeler
- Large saucepan
- Measuring cups

WHAT YOU DO

1 Prepare the vegetables first. Peel and chop the onion into small pieces. Cut the ends off the carrot, then peel and chop into small cubes. Cut the ends off the leek, then peel off the top layer and wash the leek carefully. Next, cut the leek into thin slices. Peel and cut the potato into small cubes. Cut the celery into 1-inch (2-cm) lengths.

(!) An adult should always help you when you use sharp knives and cook with boiling water, as in this recipe.

2 Heat the butter in the saucepan and fry all the vegetables, except the potatoes, for 5 minutes.

3 Stir in the flour and cook for 2 minutes.

4 Put the stock cube into the boiling water and stir until the stock cube has dissolved.

5 Add the stock water to the saucepan and bring to a boil.

6 Add the potatoes to the pan and simmer (bubble gently) for 30 minutes.

GLOSSARY

bud swelling on a plant stem that consists of overlapping young leaves or flower petals

bulb underground plant part used as a food store. Bulbs consist of overlapping fleshy leaves or scales, such as onions.

cancer disease that causes cells in a part of the body to grow out of control

carbohydrate type of nutrient we get from food. The body breaks carbohydrates down into sugars that it uses for energy.

cell all living things are made up of millions of microscopic parts called cells. Different parts of the body are made up of different types of cells.

climate normal weather patterns of a region that occur year after year

clot form a clump. Blood cells clot to stop bleeding.

crossbreed create a new breed (variety) of plant or animal by crossing two different breeds

diabetes people with diabetes are unable to turn sugars from their foods into energy, so they become very weak and tired

digestive system stomach, intestine, and other body parts that work together to break down food into pieces so small they dissolve in liquid and pass into the blood

edible safe to eat

energy people require energy to be active and to carry out all body processes, including breathing. Plants require energy from the sun to make food by photosynthesis.

explorer person who travels into unknown regions in order to learn about them

fiber part of food that cannot be digested but helps to keep the bowels working regularly

fungus plant-like organism that cannot make its own food as plants do, but instead feeds off organic matter such as dead tree trunks

liver body part located inside the body below the chest. The liver cleans the blood and produces bile, a substance that helps break down food in the digestive system.

microorganism extremely small organism that can only be seen using a microscope. Some microorganisms can cause disease or sickness.

mineral substance that comes from non-living sources such as rocks that break down and become part of the soil. Some of the nutrients that plants take in through their roots are minerals.

nutrient substance found in food that is essential for life

oxygen a gas in the air

photosynthesis process by which plants make their food

pod dry fruit that consists of a long, two-sided case to hold a plant's seeds, such as the pea pod

protein nutrient that provides the raw materials the body needs to grow and repair itself

soluble can be dissolved; for example, in a liquid or in fat

starchy something containing starch. Starch is a plant's store of excess glucose (food).

tissue group of similar cells that act together to perform a particular job. For example, skin cells form skin tissue.

tuber swollen underground stem or root used by a plant as a food store

urinate pass urine

vitamin nutrient the body needs to grow and stay healthy

whole wheat whole grain wheat. *Whole grain* means the entire seed of the grain.

FIND OUT MORE

At **www.cnpp.usda.gov**, a site from the Center for Nutrition Policy and Promotion, there is information about health and nutrition. Included is the "MyPyramid" food pyramid, which offers guidelines for a healthy, balanced diet. Explore the pyramid to find the right serving sizes for your age.

At **www.nutrition.gov**, an educational site set up by the U.S. Department of Agriculture, learn more about nutrition.

At **kidshealth.org/kid** there is a large section on staying healthy and some recipes to try.

INDEX